ROI BY DESIGN

DR. LAURA PARAMOURE

DEDICATION

To my husband, Richard, who helped make my dream of providing the ROI by Design™ model to our industry a reality by giving your unwavering commitment and engineering talents. I know without your encouragement and support this effort would not have been realized. Also, to our children, Tyler, Meghan, and Madison, who have graciously shared my attention in support of my goal. You are, without a doubt, my inspiration to be the best I can be.

TABLE OF CONTENTS

FOREWORD

When we first met back in December of 2010, I had no idea that Laura would help change the shape of our company forever. We hit it off immediately, personally and professionally, and I knew we were going to see the impact of training and development the same way. She was able to articulate the training program I had been envisioning. We worked together to see the ideas and dreams of having the best training program in our industry develop from an idea into a measureable, repeatable program with a value that can be calculated in hard dollars for my company.

I work for The Select Group, an IT and engineering recruiting firm. In an effort to respond to our rapid expansion over recent years, we've hired hundreds of recruiters and opened six new offices across the U.S and Canada. As with any growing company, we faced tremendous hurdles with onboarding and training our new recruits in a timely and effective manner. Our challenges also spanned retention, accountability, and keeping standards consistent across locations.

My vision was to create a world-class training program for all of our new hires as well as anyone promoted within our organization. In my mind, this program would ensure all of our employees were taught the same thing no matter the location or their background. Admittedly, when I first tackled this project, I had no idea where to begin. Our only instruction at the time came from a 150-page mind-numbing training manual. Although the manual contained some valuable information to anyone who could get through it, I knew it couldn't teach the vital skills necessary to produce on the job.

Our main objective and goal with the new training was to have our employees make an immediate impact on the job. Not only did I want our teams to produce better results, but I wanted a way to measure that impact directly and indirectly. Ultimately, this would prove the value we were getting out of training and show the overall impact it was having on our growth. In order to do that, our program needed to have components focused around job activities, specific skills, and overall industry knowledge. My new hires would no longer be able to "claim" they absorbed the necessary information by cruising through the manual and answering a few questions about their thoughts on the program; they would be challenged to prove their newly learned skills through testing and simulated activities in a full lifecycle of recruiting that was often more difficult than the day-to-day job duties.

Before Laura and I met, I reached out to a number of organizations nationally and locally, but none of them felt right. I ultimately leaned on my network through LinkedIn and got a recommendation to speak to eParamus (formally Strategic Training). Laura was the first person I met from the company, and from that point forward, they have been and will be a vital part of our training and development efforts. Since the beginning, we have created two robust programs using Laura's techniques and will launch numerous additional programs in years to come.

As Laura's book will tell you, the first step in this process is always analysis. One of our first meetings was a fact-finding session where Laura peeled back the layers of our metrics, documentation, standards, materials, and so on. Our team quickly discovered we had standards in our heads, but did not have them down on paper. These sessions ultimately helped us describe exactly what we wanted out of our people and what we would measure as success in the various roles. This impacted more than just training since we were able to finally describe exactly what our recruiters needed to know and the skills they needed to produce top results.

Without the information we generated in those first few meetings, Laura and her team would not have been able to help us create an impactful program. The skills and knowledge we uncovered became the foundation for the way in which we would design our program to train our people effectively. The instructional design included subject matter expert (SME)-led portions as well as student activities which helped us bridge the gap between what we were teaching and what we expected on the job. The design included specific knowledge markers and skill sets our employees needed in order to achieve their job expectations. The material was very organized which made it easy for our new hires to absorb throughout the course.

One of the keys to our success has been the evaluation process that is built into the program. Every objective we set has a teaching process as well as a method of evaluation. With pre-tests, we find out where our employees are at the outset of the training. Post-tests immediately after the training allow us to see the progress made during the sessions and help identify any individual issues that might need further attention. The transfer tests, which take place 90 days after the employee has been on the job, allow us to see if the training "took" and if our employees still retain the knowledge and skills months down the road. We use this analysis to measure not only the success of our training, but more importantly, the success of our managers in holding our employees accountable to the same standards on the job that we teach throughout the course.

The final step in the process is evaluating the results on the job. In other words, we are able to finally measure our true return on investment for training dollars and time spent. The entire program is amazing, but that part alone has been tremendous. I have since passed on the actual teaching of the course to another staff member, but I continue to use the data in executive meetings and budget sessions to prove the value in our training and development initiatives. We have employees making placements and generating revenue one week out of training. This allows our organization to continuously grow at a rate rarely seen in our industry and make an impact not only on our employees, but also on the community.

Providing a direct link from job standards to design to evaluation to results is what separates Laura and her firm from everyone else. That was a link that no other vendor understood, let alone implemented into an achievable program. Lots of companies say they measure impact, but more often than not, they are measuring how happy the employees are with the trainer or what they think they got out of the session. With our program, I have hard data that shows exactly what our new hires learned and the specific benefit it has made on our company both immediately and over time.

I have experienced the value of Laura's training methods firsthand and it has made a tremendous impact on my career and our organization. That, plus my personal relationship with Laura, is why I was thrilled and honored when she asked me to write her foreword. If you've ever struggled with securing your training budget, knowing if your training worked, and trying to capture business value for training dollars spent, I know you will find this book enlightening. I encourage you to read and study these words so you can end the struggle with determining the value of training and development for you and your business.

—Paige Goss
Director of Operations
The Select Group

INTRODUCTION: THE TRAINING INDUSTRY IDENTITY CRISIS

Working in the train-the-trainer arena, I have noticed an ongoing theme with many of my clients. They, like many training professionals, struggle with how to articulate the value of their role. Don't get me wrong! These professionals have solid skills. They love to solve problems and they know the value of learning. That's why they became training professionals in the first place.

Yet, if you ask training professionals what value their role brings to their organization, you'll get a wide array of answers. The inconsistency in their answers indicates a growing identity crisis within the training industry. I have heard trainers say their value is in knowing the latest and greatest authoring tool. Some trainers think their value is being able to quickly move huge numbers of people through training programs. Still others think their value is in being a subject matter expert in a particular topic or being a mentor to employees who are struggling in their jobs.

It is true that a training pro may do all of those things and have all those skills, but those things are not their main value to an organization. The main value of a training professional comes in identifying learning gaps in an organization and filling them. That is the value of training distilled to its essence. If we are not filling learning gaps in order to improve employee performance then we are not providing the true value of training within an organization.

But here's where the problem lies—how do you know you filled the learning gap? How do you show that value? How do you prove you were successful or show the return on investment for what you do? Ultimately, it comes down to measurement of training's impact.

A Brief History in Measuring Training

The first major focus in training measurement was introduced in 1959 when Donald Kirkpatrick examined levels of training impact. He introduced four levels of measurement.

- Reaction: What a student thinks and feels about training
- Learning: How much the student increased knowledge and skill
- Behavior Change: Did the student's behavior change due to the training
- Results: Did the organization change due to the training

Later, Jack Phillips expanded on Kirkpatrick's model by adding a fifth level. He suggested that linking business results to training is the ultimate level of evaluation. He said, "The process isn't complete until the results have been converted to monetary values and compared with the cost of the program." In other words—return on investment or ROI.

And right there is where the training industry has faltered and stagnated for 50 years. The levels were identified but never realized. Our industry has struggled with determining how to convert training results into a clear return on investment.

Here are some interesting statistics to consider: An ASTD report (2009) found that while 92% of organizations measure reaction to training, only 36% believe that's an effective measure. In addition, nearly 60% believed ROI to have high value, but only 18% measured training on that level.

This research shows a clear disconnect between what businesses want and need from training and what training professionals are providing.

Why Training Measurement Matters

The only way to gather data for training ROI is to measure training. However, in order to effectively measure we must first clarify which training measurements are important. What training data do stakeholders find useful? What shows return on investment for training in an organization?

Some organizations are content to know the cost of training and how many courses were produced for that cost. Others want to know that the participants (or their managers or both) thought the training was appropriate, useful, and applied. Both types of data may be valid, but do they accurately portray training value to an organization? Is your training budget secure because you taught a certain number of courses? Is it secure because participants and their managers said the training was helpful? The likely answer to these questions is no.

To find the real value of training we must ask what the organization needs from the training function. What is the training product? What should the end result of training be?

Most executives responsible for the training budget say that the work of training is to provide courses that will educate and prepare employees, making them more effective and more productive on the job. So, if a more productive employee is the goal, then what is it about training that provides that end result?

Let's consider what service/product training provides to prepare employees. The *ASTD Training and Development Handbook* (written by the American Society for Training & Development) says that training can impact knowledge, skills, or attitudes. Contrary to what some believe, a training program cannot change your personality, your morals, or make you more likable. Instead, a training program helps you acquire new knowledge and skills so you can perform better on the job. Therefore, if the goal of training is to acquire new knowledge and skills, how is this accomplished? What mechanism does the trainer use to accomplish this goal? What is the product that training provides to accomplish this goal? Simply put, **the training product is the design and facilitation of a training program.**

The main mechanism for increasing knowledge and skills is the design of a program that enables the participant to learn and apply new content. The main skill (and business value) of a trainer is the ability to understand how adults learn and how to design a program that results in learning. Trainers must determine the content needed to improve performance and the most effective ways to deliver that content to ensure comprehension. Both the program content and content delivery manifest in the training design. Therefore, it is the training design that dictates the effectiveness of instruction and determines the success of acquiring new knowledge and skills.

When we recognize that the training product is an effectively designed program, measurement becomes much easier. Why? Because the goal of an effectively designed program is to acquire knowledge or skills, and we know how to measure the acquisition of knowledge and skills. Trainers can easily determine if the content of the program was appropriate for the knowledge and skill used on the job, and if the combination of the program design and the training delivery resulted in performance improvement. Specifically, we know knowledge gain can be assessed with a knowledge test, and skill gain can be assessed by a change in behavior.

Understanding the training product and how to measure the results of that product are the keys to improving the training profession. By ensuring the tangible outputs of training are measured and understood, the training profession eliminates the ambiguity around training's impact or value to an organization.

The Cost of Not Measuring Is Too High

The lack of providing an appropriate measure of training impact has become increasingly evident and the need for viable measurement is growing more important. Businesses now insist on seeing the hard data that ties a monetary value to training. In fact, for training professionals the cost of NOT measuring training impact has been very high. There is far too much ambiguity around the value of training to organizations. This misperception about value has shown up in many ways—as subject matter experts (SMEs) being used as designers, as cuts in training personnel, and as reductions in training budgets. If you're a training professional, you know exactly what I'm talking about. When times get tough, you wonder how long it'll take before your budget hits the chopping block.

Currently, many training professionals find it hard to prove the value of training to an organization. Why? They do not know how to show training success in concrete terms. Measurement is the key to making that link.

We know if our industry ever hopes to be seen as a strategic business partner, we must first understand our own value. Then, we must know how to communicate that value in business terms, as hard proof of achieved goals—as dollars and cents that add to the bottom line.

After 30 years of working in business, 15 of which were in the training profession, I have a strong passion for improving the reputation of training and its contribution to an organization. This book represents years of practice in improving instructional design and providing concrete evidence of the value of training.

This effort is intended to show how using best practices in our training product (training design) helps align the training function to business goals. It will show how you can easily generate proof of impact. It will describe using Measurable Instructional Design™ to make a training product that can be measured, and show how and when to evaluate training in order to support organizational goals and highlight training value.

Some details of the steps in the ROI by Design™ model are provided to support understanding of the process. However, the goal of this book is not to teach the steps but instead to provide the "what" and "why" of using the ROI by Design™ model to support reaching the goal of improving our industry's reputation and showing the real impact of training.

References

ASTD, "The value of evaluation: Making training evaluation more effective." (Alexandria, VA: ASTD Press, 2009).

Chief Learning Officer Magazine, "Chief learning officer executive research brief: Learning outlook 2013." Unpublished report. (Chicago: MediaTec Publishing, 2012).

Training Magazine, Donna Goldwasser, "Beyond ROI." (Volume 38, Bill Communications, Inc. 2001).

Jack J. Phillips, "Accountability in human resource management." (Houston: Gulf Publishing, 1996).

1

ANALYSIS

Instructional Design

The corporate training world is overflowing with professionals who entered the field without formal instructional design training. Many came into training because they were subject matter experts (SMEs) in their companies and their employer needed training created on the subject in which they were experts. Others entered the field because they were proficient in technology and could easily use the latest authoring tools. Still others came from a public education background and wanted to leave it behind for the business field.

The preponderance of people entering the field who are not formally educated in the training discipline paired with the inability to measure training outputs has contributed to the identity crisis within the training profession. With many practitioners uneducated in formal instructional design, there is a shortage of those who understand the science behind instructional design and there are limitations to the understanding of how training supports businesses.

The connection between training and other business functions can be murky. For most training professionals, the common language used to explain training's outputs focuses on learning objectives. Unfortunately, learning objectives do not always translate well into the business terms typically used by other stakeholders in an organization. The disconnect between what trainers describe as training outcomes and what organizations identify as business goals has been highlighted in recent years. Progressive organizations have begun to recognize that alignment between training and business objectives is essential for success. Designing training programs to support and improve business goals begins with the ability to find a common language and incorporate business goals into design.

The most common model used for instructional design is the ADDIE model. The ADDIE model is a Systems Approach to Training, or SAT, that was developed in 1975 by Florida State University to support military training. It is the most highly accepted model for Instructional Systems Design (ISD). (ISD is the process of creating training that helps learners acquire a knowledge or skill in a way that is effective, efficient, and appealing.) ADDIE is an acronym describing the process of instructional design and development. It is a comprehensive five-phase process that provides a guideline for building effective training. Many practitioners have added to or modified the ADDIE model, but the typical five phases of the model include:

<u>A</u>nalysis: Analyze the situation to identify gaps in performance that can be impacted by training and to determine the goals of instruction.

Design: Design the instructional plan to meet learner needs.

Development: Develop content and learning materials based on the plan created in the design phase.

Implementation: Put the plan into action. The learning created is put into the environment in which it is going to be used.

Evaluation: Evaluate the learning. Determine if the learning accomplished the goals set during the analysis phase.

The popularity and longevity of the ADDIE model shows that training professionals find this model to be a good foundation for the training process. This model shows all of the major steps and considerations for producing training. It includes the up-front analysis and the back-end evaluation to support a closed loop solution to training programs. However, like most popular models, it is not without its criticisms. Two of the major criticisms of the model have been:

- The analysis examines learning requirements but not the requirements of the business.
- The evaluation measures the learning but not how the organization is impacted by the learning.

These criticisms make way for a new model that incorporates business requirements and an improved way to measure learning results and impact to an organization.

A New Model—Measurable Instructional Design™

Analysis

KPM/CM
metric to be
impacted by
training

Job Requirements
skills on the job
that will impact
the KPM

TRAINING OBJECTIVES
OBSERVABLE
PERFORMANCE
OUTCOMES

Instructional
Strategies
methods and
exercises to
achieve objectives

Mastery Test
evaluation of
student's mastery

Measurable Instructional Design™ (MID) is a new model that speaks to the major components of the ADDIE model and answers some of the main criticisms of the ADDIE model. MID makes alignment between training outputs and business objectives a cornerstone of design. Like ADDIE, the MID model begins by analyzing the problem that led to the request for training. However, the MID model enhances the ADDIE approach by teaching instructional designers to collaborate with business unit managers in the analysis. Together, the business manager and the trainer identify learning requirements using business terms. Specifically, the business manager and trainer work together to identify key performance metrics (KPMs) that are used to measure effective performance.

Almost all business managers have certain things (indicators) they review to determine if the areas they manage are running appropriately. These indicators are often referred to as metrics. Metrics can measure the results of a process, behavior, or a combination of both. In the MID model the trainer learns to work with the manager to determine the metric that reflects the results of a key performance in the company. Improvement in the key performance metric becomes the goal of the training and the foundation for the design.

The MID model uses business requirements as instructional goals. This model then defines performance standards that impact the KPM. In other words, aligning training objectives to business outcomes begins the process.

I know what you are thinking—training professionals have always considered business goals when developing training. I agree. The main difference is that with the MID model, the training professional learns how to support the manager in identifying the **business measurement**. The trainer educates the business unit manager on how the training will improve performance using standards of performance as a gage. This collaboration and alignment starts with the training request.

The Training Request

A training request normally launches the development of any training program. Training professionals often use the training request as the impetus to analyze the problem that led to the request. Traditionally, training professionals talk in terms of goals, objectives, and the process for the training program. They determine the content needed to achieve the goals outlined by the business manager. In truth, business managers and trainers usually collaborate on the goals of the program, but rarely do they identify or discuss the operational metric that has not been performing as expected and eventually led to the training request.

Since business managers often use operational metrics to help them identify a problem, their goal for requesting training is centered on improvement to a metric. For instance, if a technical call center manager typically sees 5 errors out of every 100 orders processed, but begins to see 20 or 30 errors for every 100 orders processed, the manager looks for reasons for the errors. The manager may conclude that there is a need for training to "fix" the problem. Traditionally, the trainer (if given the chance) starts an analysis to determine if the problem is due to something training can fix. If it is, then the trainer would develop content for the training program.

In order to develop content for the program, trainers usually start by discussing training goals and objectives, and then move quickly to developing the training programs. Trainers have rarely been taught how to address the connection between learning and business objectives. Therefore many trainers don't know how to discuss the problem using terms that are recognizable to business managers. Having worked with hundreds of companies, I rarely see trainers who are well versed in determining what metric indicates success or verifying that an improvement in performance will impact the metric. This is an important missing piece in the traditional ADDIE model.

A training request usually happens due to a perceived business need. Historically, the business unit requesting training views the training professional as a producer and not a business partner. Business managers think in terms of performance and typically request a course based on the **subject** for which they think they need training. Trainers think in terms of learning goals and objectives and communicate with the manager in these terms. The training outcome envisioned by these two stakeholders is often not the same because they do not speak the same language! Business managers focus on performance outcomes and training professionals focus on learning outcomes. For example, if there are errors in the processing of orders in the call center and the number of orders processed in a period of time is decreasing, the trainer may create a learning objective such as:

- The student will identify the correct pricing for each of the items ordered from the customer.

   Or:

- The student will know the expected time to complete an order form per customer.

The business manager does not think in terms of the building blocks of learning. He or she would typically view outputs from a higher level and would only consider the goal of the program to be:

- Students should be able to complete all of the fields in the order form quickly and correctly.

In the manager's mind, if the students are able to do this then the metric being reviewed would improve. The changes in behavior that will impact the metric and the metric change itself are what the manager looks for to assess the results of training.

How can we connect learning and performance objectives? The MID model teaches us that the intersection between learning and performance is in the instructional design process.

If trainers learn to work with the training requester to reach agreement on the operational metric that will be measured for success _and_ collaborate on the standards of performance needed to address the metric, the chances of training success greatly increase. Aligning metrics and standards enables both stakeholders to be held accountable for their influence on improvements to the identified KPM.

Determining the KPM

During the MID process, trainers work with the training requester to determine the proper metric. If you read the current research on training analytics, you will often hear the experts say that training should be linked to metrics such as customer satisfaction or revenue generated.  These are very high-level metrics. For years, the experts in training measurement have tried to connect training results to these types of metrics. They have tried using complicated mathematical methods to isolate training impact from all of the other things that influence the metric. The goal of isolation was to determine what part training played in any changes to the metric. Unfortunately, this thinking is misguided and impractical for the business environment. No one has the time, money, or even the desire to hire everyone who would be needed to accurately isolate all of the influences to these high-level metrics and make that measurement.

More important, no other function in business attempts to show value in this way. The more practical solution is to determine the metric that can be ***directly*** influenced by a training program. Instead of trying to connect training to strategic metrics (which are influenced by several things), choose the operational metric that can be directly influenced by behavior change.

If you consider that training is designed to impact knowledge, skills, or attitudes, then the only reasonable conclusion would be to determine the metric that can be influenced by changes in these areas. Since gains in knowledge and skills create behavior change, a metric that measures behavior is the only direct tie to training. Strategic metrics—such as retention rates, employee satisfaction, customer satisfaction, costs of goods sold, and profit—are influenced by several factors and are not good indicators of training success. You would need to spend a tremendous amount of time and money trying to isolate the impact of various factors, and your results would be educated guesses at best if you used these types of metrics! Operational metrics (or more specifically, KPMs which are measured at the operational level) are already being used by business to determine the health of an organization. In fact, they are often the tool the business manager uses to identify the need for training. The problem is they are just not being communicated to the trainer or tied to training design.

Breaking down information into actionable items is not new to business. Well run manufacturing plants have been doing this for years. Manufacturing plants often identify Key Performance Indicators (KPIs) that reflect the desired results of each part of their manufacturing process. They look at the processes that are used, the results that are achieved, and adjust when there is a discrepancy. Any company that hopes to maintain competitiveness, grow, and succeed, needs to identify performance standards in all areas of their business.

Many high performing organizations seek out designations such as the ISO 9000 for businesses, or Magnet status for hospitals.

Attaining these designations requires them to identify standards of performance and measure themselves to ensure the achievement of those standards. Tools such as Six Sigma or concepts like lean manufacturing are designed around this same rigorous notion. In fact, all of the organizations I have worked with have identified at least some level of performance or output necessary for success in their business. For example, metrics are often determined in three different ways: for individuals (used in performance reviews), team or department levels (used to measure team or department success), and organizational levels (used to gauge strategic success). The specific metrics used are determined by the type of business, the department, and the culture of the organization. Operational metrics typically address production outputs, quality requirements, and process results within the different departments of an organization. Without an identified level of production, quality, and performance, organizations struggle to know how well they are doing. Specifically, without measuring metrics of some type, an organization does not have a means to know where improvement is needed to request training!

The first part of analysis in the MID process involves identifying the KPM and verifying that the change to that KPM can be achieved through a change in knowledge, skill, or attitude for a group within the organization. The second part of analysis focuses on the standards of performance that are needed to impact the KPM.

Standards of Performance (Job Requirements)

If someone asks if there are standards of performance for the jobs and processes within their organization, the likely response would be "of course." Most agree that without standards of performance, goals and objectives could not be

Job Requirements
skills on the job
that will impact
the KPM

met. Unfortunately, in the world of training, these "standards" are not always evident. Organizations are often so focused on making the product, providing the service, and keeping customers happy that they do not take the time to agree upon (much less document) their performance standards. When business managers review operational metrics they rarely have written standards that outline expected behaviors. The standards may be clear in the minds of management, but often they are not written down to allow for an agreement on performance.

Identifying and documenting standards is vital to addressing performance, impacting a performance metric, and measuring the success of training. Performance standards provide the trainer with the content for the training program, provide both the trainer and business manager a way to determine success in training, and provide the learner with a reference for performance. Therefore, developing job requirements and standards of performance is the second stage of analysis.

After the second step of analysis has been completed, the direction of the training program often changes because agreement to standards clarifies the problem. The collaborative process that occurs when standards are created allows for redefining and changing the old methods of performance. Making this second step a part of the training process helps align training efforts with business needs. In addition, requiring alignment between the trainer and business manager on the standards of performance and the means of measurement (KPM) ensures that training dollars are spent on something that the organization agrees is necessary for performance improvement. Taking time to agree on standards supports the basic components needed for organizational growth and provides good benchmarks for measurement of training success and job performance. It has been my experience that the second stage of analysis in the MID process is an important tool to be used to improve the effectiveness of any organization, not just training programs.

Sources for Standards

Standards for training contain specific requirements for job performance and can typically be found when examining company documents such as:

- Manuals or handbooks
- SOPs (standard operating procedures) or WP (working practices)
- Written policies or procedures
- Job descriptions

These documents not only provide the types of performance needed, they often deliver the conditions under which the performance will be made, and at what level the performance needs to be completed. These details of performance are used to create measureable training objectives. Once job requirements are clarified, stakeholders can agree on the course outcomes and the ability of the outcomes to address the identified KPM.

Many of our clients tell us that the step of agreeing on metrics and developing standards is a tremendous value to them. Training design professionals are typically very proficient at breaking down large amounts of material and distilling the information into manageable chunks. This same process is used in the development of standards. Standards reflect the tasks that need to be completed and the level of completion. For instance, if you are conducting a training course on stress management for an organization, you would determine the type of information on stress that needs to be learned in order to improve performance. You would consider the job environment, the necessary information on stress, and the desired result to create the content (the standard you are using) to accomplish the goal. Agreement between the trainer and the manager on the standard(s) that will accomplish the desired result provides the foundation for the course and provides the conditions and criteria for measuring success.

Connecting the KPM to the Training Goal

Once the business manager and the trainer agree upon the KPM (the organizational metric), both stakeholders know the end goal. Once they identify (or create) the standard, then they agree on what is needed to accomplish the goal. But, how do you connect the organizational goal to the training goal?

First, let's define organizational and training goals:

- An organizational goal is a change in the organizational indicator (KPM) that is used to determine the results of a process or a task.
- A training goal states the desired outcome of training.

To connect the KPM to the training goal you need to state (at a high level) the outcome of training that will impact the KPM. In other words, the training goal aligns with what the KPM measures. In our previous example, our KPM may be measuring the number of errors in call center order processing. Our training goal may be "prepare customer service representatives to process orders with less than a five percent error rate." Alignment between the KPM and the training goal highlights the intent of the stakeholders. The trainers produce a program with the stated goal and the achievement of that stated goal will result in performance changes that will impact the KPM. This alignment is why it is important to start with the KPM.

In a more complicated example, perhaps a business manager requests training because he has received an increase in complaints from customers stating that customer service representatives are rude. The business manager recognizes that a surge in workload has increased the stress level of employees. The manager determines that stress reduction would improve their performance. The manager requests a training course on managing stress. The KPM in this example is the customer complaints about employee phone etiquette. This is a metric that the manager tracks and uses to manage the department. The manager has determined that the increased stress of the employees has led to them being rude to the customers and created a rise in customer complaints. To address the KPM, the goal of this training program may be to "perform stress reducing techniques while manning the customer service desk."

It is important that the training goal reflects what the KPM measures. In this example, the business manager determined the need for a stress management course. The course goal is to provide stress management techniques that can be used on the job. If that training goal is realized then, when training is complete, the impact of stress management knowledge and skills will be tested against the ability to change the performance measured by the KPM of customer complaints. Once the expected behavior change (students using their stress reducing techniques on the job) is measured, the stakeholders will know if the expected behavior change occurred. If it did, then the stakeholders can look to see if the change in behavior created the expected change in the KPM.

In analysis, the trainer and business manager collaborate to determine the KPM and consider all behaviors which may impact the KPM in order to determine the course content. There are many ways to address training analysis. The analysis of the problem helps to narrow down the potential knowledge or skill deficiency. Identifying the KPM (which reveals the behavior results) is the means to connect behavior changes to organizational measurements. Selection of the KPM does not replace the need to do analysis; it is simply an added step in analysis.

If the selected KPM measures the results of behavior change, and if both the business manager and the trainer agree on the KPM and training goal, then when a course is measured for success we can **test the validity of the assumptions made in the process**. We will know if the increase in knowledge and skills in stress management solved the problem. Wouldn't it be nice to determine if the decisions we make in running our business are accurate? Think of what we could do if we learned from our mistakes and could incorporate our learning to improve our ability to do our jobs. Imagine how great it would be to learn the training strategies that worked and those that did not. Imagine eventually being able to predict the organizational results from training because you have a history of data to show you what works and what doesn't! The alignment of the KPM to the training goal, and the resulting measures, will allow this to happen.

Connecting the Training Goal to the Training Objectives

Once the KPM and goal of the training course are aligned, things become very clear. An instructional designer typically starts with the agreed upon goal of a course, which tells the designer what the learners need to learn. The next step is to identify the objectives that must be met in order to get there.

In our technical call center error example, the goal is to reduce errors (and the KPM is the measurement of the amount of errors). The objectives might include learning about the different types of errors, or how to avoid them. If performance standards are identified then the types of objectives needed would be evident because we know that the standards reflect the best practices that achieve desired outcomes. We know the standards we need to meet in order to impact the performance that the KPM measures. Instructional designers then need to review the agreed upon standards, and use those standards to create objectives that support the training goal.

When a KPM or goal is connected to a set of standards, the trainer knows what type or level of performance has to be met in order to improve the KPM. Connecting the goal of training to the objectives in the course will essentially map out a set of steps necessary to reach the goal. When we develop training objectives based on the stated standards of performance, then we know we will be able to impact the KPM because the KPM is the measure of success of the performance.

Design Sequencing

Like most instructional design models, the MID process includes design sequencing. This means the trainer organizes objectives in a way that will guide learners through the course in a logical manner. How well the learners grasp the course concepts is dictated by the skill of the instructional designer in applying adult learning theory to design sequencing.

With the MID process, designers start with a KPM, determine the standards of behavior measured by the KPM, develop a goal to address the KPM, and create objectives that will reach the goal. Connecting these steps is powerful in producing training that can change performance. This logical progression helps the instructional designer start with a clear understanding of necessary outputs and also makes it much easier to sequence the material to achieve expected results.

Behavior to Results

The title of this book is *ROI by Design*. It was named after the concept that ROI in training can be achieved through measurement of the design of training. The key component of the ROI by Design™ measurement model is that training impact is measured by behavior change. Learning is measured by the specific knowledge or skill gained in the course, the application of those skills, and the changes made to the organizational metrics by that application. As we have discussed in this section, analysis that reviews behavior change that is linked to job performance, and the metrics that measure job performance, allows instructional designers to create a program that is targeted for business impact.

By measuring behavior change and the results of behavior change, both at the individual and class levels, we can determine if knowledge and skills were gained in training, if students applied the new behaviors on the job, and if the application of the behaviors changed the metrics used to measure performance. Fundamentally, we also measure the training professional's ability to work with the business manager to design and facilitate a program that enables a behavior change. What is important is that we measure behavior change—not the perception of behavior change, but the **actual** behavior changes that impact business metrics. After all, isn't that what training is all about?

Case Study – The Select Group – The Beginning

The Select Group is an IT and Engineering recruiting firm headquartered in Raleigh NC. They have offices across the US and have grown rapidly over the past several years. Recent accolades include the Staffing Industry Analyst's 2011 and 2012 list of Fastest Growing Staffing Firms, 2010 Triangle Business Journal Fast 50, and INC. 5000.

Their growth rate meant onboarding new recruiting staff at a rapid clip. To keep pace, they needed to replace their outdated training program with one more attuned to the actual recruiting process. The purpose of the new program was to quickly train new hires to make them capable of successful recruiting from day one. The business impact of the training program had to be quantified. They engaged eParamus™ (formerly Strategic Training) to develop the program.

To begin, eParamus™ sat down with The Select Group and helped them define their goals. A fact finding session was conducted to determine the objectives they wanted to achieve and the standards of performance they wanted to use. In that process it was discovered that the standards of performance were mainly in the heads of the leadership of this fast growing company. The Select Group identified metrics for measuring the performance of the role but documentation on how to achieve the performance was limited.

Using the framework for on-the-job execution and the metrics used to measure on-the-job performance, a detailed set of standards was generated. The standards became the standard operating procedures for the recruiter role.

The specific metrics against which the effectiveness of the training program was measured included all of the things that a new recruiter had to do to succeed in their job. The new recruiters needed to intelligently speak to candidates during the recruiting cycle. The Select Group wanted their recruiters to manage their candidates through the recruiting pipeline. Recruiters needed to know how to generate leads, build and maintain relationships, coach people on how to interview, and qualify potential recruits against a desired skill set.

The rigorous onboarding program was designed based on on-the job execution. It centered around skill and knowledge transfer based on the specific metrics identified by The Select Group. Defining standards and determining metrics was the first step of the process before proceeding to the Design phase.

DESIGN

In the ROI by Design™ methodology, training programs can be measured because they are designed to be measured. The Measurable Instruction Design™ (MID) process guides instructional designers in creating training that is measurable. By following the MID model for instructional design, trainers can measure how well students learned in the classroom, if a student's behavior changed on the job, and how the training program impacted the organization.

What is it about the MID process that makes training measurable at these levels? It starts in the analysis phase of design. That phase focuses on two major steps which ensure collaboration between the trainers and the business managers and results in the identification of the key business indicators (metrics) that showed there was a problem. In analysis, the business manager and the trainer agree that a change in the key performance metric (KPM) reflects the ultimate goal of the training program. In order to impact a KPM, the next step in analysis is to identify the standards of performance that, when achieved, have the ability to impact the KPM. Performance standards provide the trainer with the content needed to develop training and further align the business manager and trainer on the required conditions and criteria of performance.

Pinpointing organizational needs and agreeing on standards are the steps in MID analysis that begin the process for making training measureable. The steps in the design phase of MID continue the process by identifying objectives that will support the goals that were determined in the analysis phase.

What Makes Training Measureable

Before we consider the design steps that make training measurable, let's consider what makes anything measurable. In order for something to be measurable there must be three things.

1. A method of measurement that is easy to complete.
2. A way for the results to be computed (observed).
3. A consistent and repeatable method for measuring.

To say it succinctly, for something to be measurable, it needs to be easy to measure, easy to observe, and easy to repeat.

Keeping those things in mind, let's consider training. The first thing we need is an easy way to complete training measurement. The training industry consistently uses knowledge and skills tests and end-of-course surveys to assess training. The popularity of these methods clearly demonstrates that they are easy to complete.

The second requirement is to have a means for the results to be computed (observed). In training, the goal is to increase knowledge or skill and improve job performance. Therefore, we need an observable means to see knowledge or skill gain. Currently, we can measure an increase in knowledge through a knowledge test and the acquisition of skills through a skills test, so that meets our second requirement for measurement.

The final need is the ability to repeat the measurement. If we use knowledge and skills tests then we can easily repeat those tests. Repeating a knowledge and skill test is common practice, especially with today's technology.

So, can training be measured? Absolutely.

The real challenge in measuring training does not come from having methods to measure (criteria one) or a repeatable process (criteria three). The challenge comes in having a clear and concrete way to observe and compute the knowledge acquisition and skills gains.

Training professionals who are proficient in instructional design know how to create observable results. The largest professional organization for training is the American Society for Training and Development (ASTD). ASTD has supported using best practices in instructional design for years. Those best practices include aligning instruction with business goals and insisting on clarity in design, both of which are required for measurable training. The problem has been with adoption of these best practices. There has been a lack of knowledge across the profession regarding the steps of instructional design that align instruction with business goals and the steps necessary to achieve clarity in design. Without adequate measures, training professionals have been unable to see which parts of their design have been effective or ineffective. Unfortunately the lack of a way to measure programs has led to a common practice of designing programs that are not measurable!

The key to clarity in design is in the way course objectives are written. How many times have you taken a training course with ambiguous objectives such as "understand Excel" or "know how to give feedback" or even "be aware of policy"? Each of these is an example of something that cannot be measured. That is because they are stated in terms so broad that no one observes (at least in the same way) when they are complete. Without clear parameters those that observe the behavior will have to rely on their own interpretation of the conditions of performance or the level of performance required for the task.

Creating Measurable Objectives

For a training program to meet the second criteria for measurement (a way for the item to be computed or observed), it must contain measurable objectives. *A measurable objective is an objective that is clearly defined so the outcomes can be quantified.* The concept of creating measurable objectives is not new to the training profession. Best practices in the development of objectives have always included a performance, a condition, and a criterion. The inclusion of these factors makes them measurable.

Without formal instructional design training, many instructional designers have defaulted to making general objectives. A general objective often tells the expected performance (in general terms). General objectives provide the content area addressed in training and often leave the details of the performance up to interpretation. This interpretation leads to ambiguity in expected results and can often lead to content in a course that does not directly address the performance issue.

Unlike general objectives, a measureable objective includes the required performance, conditions of performance, and criteria of

24

successful performance allowing for a very specific outcome. These three create an objective that can become the cornerstone of what to teach, how to teach it, and how to measure the success of what was taught.

Objectives without these factors are left to interpretation. If a trainer writes an objective such as "the student will understand Excel," what does that mean? Will the student understand the purpose of Excel, the formulas used in Excel, or perhaps how to manipulate columns in Excel? Who knows? The objective is ambiguous and therefore cannot be measured. When business managers want to fill a performance gap, they think in terms of the end result of the training. It is the trainer's job to identify what students need to learn in Excel to achieve the desired results. They need to determine what performance (what specific knowledge or skill in using Excel) is needed so they can design the course to meet the required result. The instructional designer communicates the rigor of the course through the objectives.

Any ambiguity in what needs to be taught is removed when the stakeholders in training clearly understand the performance needed, the conditions under which the performance needs to happen, and at what level the performance needs to be accomplished. As we discussed earlier, when there is a request for training, business managers often look at a KPM that shows job performance is not as it should be. The business manager requests training in an attempt to improve a KPM through an improvement in performance. The training program goal would be to improve the skills that impact the KPM. Course objectives are designed to achieve a behavior change that, in turn, achieves the goal of the course. When the goal is reached, it will be reflected in an improved KPM.

In our previous example where a technical call center's error rate increased in order processing, the business manager may determine that the call center representatives are not using Excel properly, which is leading to increased errors. The KPM is the number of errors per order. The goal is to reduce the errors in processing orders using Excel and the objectives are the specific tasks necessary to use Excel effectively.

Each measureable objective would address the identified gap in knowledge and skill in using Excel on the job. Perhaps the objective would look something like this: "Students will be able to create formula 'X' using three columns and arriving at 'y' result." This objective can be easily understood by both the manager and the trainer, it can be easily viewed against the standard of performance, and it can be easily measured through observing the students' ability to complete.

Linking Measurable Objectives to Instructional Strategies

In the typical instructional design process, the course goal is determined and then a set of objectives to achieve the goal is generated. Once training objectives that are necessary to meet the training goal have been created, it is time to determine the instructional strategies or teaching 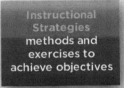 methods that will accomplish the objectives. Choosing the best instructional strategy to ensure learners are able to acquire the needed knowledge and skill is a key competency of the instructional designer.

Determining the most effective instructional strategies, as well as the best way to evaluate an objective, requires the specificity of a measureable objective.

Training professionals know there are a number of different instructional strategies that can be used to support knowledge or skill gain. Instructional strategies that can be used to address knowledge may include:

- Readings
- Small group discussions
- Question and answer sessions
- Lectures
- Demonstrations
- Discussions

Instructional strategies to learn a skill may include:

- Guided observations
- Demonstrations
- Simulations
- Role play
- Case studies
- Games

Instructional designers choose strategies to address what needs to be learned and the level at which it needs to be learned. Unfortunately, instructional strategies that enable a quick way to convey information and are easy to create have become the default. The most widely used instructional strategy today is lecture accompanied by PowerPoint slides. Without consideration of the need to acquire or apply knowledge to a certain level, trainers have little motivation to use other instructional strategies. In addition, without the ability to measure success in achieving objectives, there is little motivation to change methods.

When working with measurable objectives, we are exposed to the need to reevaluate the use of methods such as lecture. Using measureable objectives, we know the conditions of performance and the level of performance that are required. This helps us determine the instructional strategies that are most effective to achieve the desired result. If we consider performance conditions and performance level required, we may recognize that showing the information on a PowerPoint slide and reading slide content to students may not be enough!

Let's consider the following example:

- Course KPM: Reduce customer complaints of rudeness.
- Course goal: Provide stress management techniques to use at the customer service desk.
- General course objective: The student will know stress reducing techniques.
- Measurable course objective: When working the call center desk, the student demonstrates the 30-second stress reducing technique, including all the steps in the correct order.

The general course objective is not measurable. The objective tells what the student will know in general terms: the student will know stress reducing techniques. The measurable course objective, however, specifically identifies what the student will know. In the measurable objective, we know the objective is for students to be aware of the technique while operating in their work environment. We know they need to be able to use the 30-second technique while on the job, and we know the students will learn to execute all steps of the technique in the proper order. It is much easier to determine if the objective is achieved when it provides this level of detail.

When an instructional designer designs around a general objective, the content of the course can be quite varied. The instructional designer could provide a variety of information on stress reducing techniques without regard to the targeted goal. The trainer could "teach" the content by simply conveying information on stress reducing techniques and call it a day! With a general objective, there is little motivation to instruct in any way other than just conveying information. This is because without clarity on what business goal needs to be reached or specifics of the performance needed, the instructional strategies used in the program become less important. Typically, when a course is taught based on a general objective, the stakeholders are at first satisfied because they received the course on stress techniques that they asked for. However, when the stakeholder does not see a change in performance or a change in the KPM they begin to complain that training was ineffective. We have all experienced times when the content requested was delivered in the training course, and the job performance changed little, if at all. General objectives often lead to unsatisfied stakeholders because the goals of the business manager were not clearly identified, targeted, or reached.

When objectives are measurable they enable both the training professional and the business manager to clearly understand what the student needs to learn from training and to agree on the specific performance objectives that will reach the intended business goal. In our example, the measurable objective helps the instructional designer to know what instructional strategy to use to reinforce the timing of the stress reducing technique and what strategy will enable the student to absorb all steps in the process.

The conditions of the objective reflect the job environment in which students will be using the knowledge. The criterion reflects the extent of knowledge or skill needed for them to apply the learning on the job. Students likely need more than a PowerPoint presentation that gives a list of steps in order to recall and use the 30-second stress reducing technique while they are at the customer service desk. At the very least, students should have a knowledge objective that gives them the specific knowledge needed to apply the skill. Ideally the instructional designer would include both a knowledge objective that enables the learner to know the steps and would include a skill objective to have them practice the skill.

Instructional strategies, such as a small group discussion that focuses on the opportunity to use the technique on the job, along with the steps to complete the technique, would be an effective means for students to absorb the necessary stress reducing technique. Or, a demonstration and discussion may be the best means for the student to learn the material. No matter which strategy is chosen, knowing the performance conditions and performance criteria gives the instructional designer the information needed to design the course.

Soft Skills

Almost without fail when I am speaking to groups someone will ask about designing for or measuring soft skills. In addition, many times when reading forums or blogs on training I see someone who contends that soft skills cannot be measured. When people tell me that they believe soft skills cannot be measured, I ask them this question: If soft skills cannot be measured then what are they teaching in a soft skills course? What knowledge are they providing or what skill are they developing? In short, if soft skills can be taught then they can be measured.

The concern for measuring soft skills is often centered on the quantification of the soft skill. How do you quantify a soft skill? Let's consider the example of the soft skill of communication. Many organizations want their managers to be able to communicate well especially when they are working with employees or doing something like providing performance feedback. They want managers to show good listening skills and professional communication. The important thing to remember is that soft skills, just like technical skills, have standards of behavior. Standards of behavior can be measured. For instance, what reflects good listening skills? What behaviors are you looking for? Perhaps the behavior you want to encourage is not interrupting, nodding your head, or keeping eye contact. Communication, like any other skill, has standards of behavior. It is those standards of behavior that should be conveyed and practiced in the course. Once standards are determined, that becomes the content of the course. The soft skill standards, just like technical skill standards, are paramount to adding clarity to what behaviors will be expected in order to deem training as successful. After all, it is the observation of these behaviors (or lack of observation of these behaviors) that the stakeholders will use to measure the success of your program.

Remember, training can impact knowledge, skills, or attitudes. It cannot make a manager a nicer person. If the manager knows what to do and shows through exercises in the course that he or she can display the soft skill, then training is successful. If after the course, the manager chooses not to use the skill on the job then that is another issue. It is no longer a training issue. Reinforcing what training can and cannot fix with a gap in performance is important. Soft skills fall under the same rules as technical skills with regard to what training can do. If addressing the gap requires a knowledge, skill, or attitude change, then whether it is a soft skill or a technical skill it can be measured. If it is not knowledge, skill, or attitude change that is needed, then it is not a training issue.

Linking Measurable Objectives to Knowledge or Skill Mastery

Just as the measurable objective provides information necessary to determine a good instructional strategy, it also provides vital information on the best way to measure the objective. Measurement of a knowledge objective may include the following types of mastery questions:

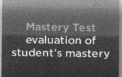

Mastery Test
evaluation of
student's mastery

- Multiple choice
- True/false
- Open ended
- Checklist
- Ranking scales
- Essay

Measurement of a skill objective may include:

- Scenarios
- Role play
- Demonstrations
- Observations
- Simulations

The type of question you use to measure your objective is directly related to the condition and criteria of the objective. To continue our example:

- Course KPM: Reduce customer complaints of rudeness.
- Course goal: Provide stress management techniques.
- General course objectives:
  - The student will know stress reducing techniques (knowledge objective).
  - The student will use stress reducing techniques (skill objective).
- Measureable course objectives:
  - When working the call center desk, the student knows the 30-second stress reducing technique, including all the steps in the correct order (knowledge objective).
  - In between taking calls, the student displays the 30-second stress reducing technique with all of the steps completed in order (skill objective).

For knowledge objectives, you need to consider how detailed or how in-depth a student needs to understand the material to achieve the objective. For instance, does the student need to immediately recall the information or will the student have the benefit of a job aid to help recall the information when needed? Do students need to recognize the answer or do they need to produce the information without prompting? Answers to these questions are found in the stated condition (when working at the call center desk). The knowledge is needed when they are working at their desk so we can decide if a job aid is available or not. Regardless, the condition helps identify the type of evaluation because it provides the parameters for success. If students only need to recognize the correct information, then perhaps a multiple choice question is sufficient. If students need to understand a concept, perhaps an open-ended question is the best way to test retention. In our example, the student needs to know the right technique to use (the 30-second technique) and needs to know all of the steps in order (the criteria). A multiple-choice question may be sufficient to determine knowledge of the correct technique, but a checklist may be needed if students are to list the steps in order.

In our skill objective, the student needs to be able to use the technique in an environment with limited time available. Perhaps a role play that simulates the customer service environment would be best. Or a demonstration/observation would enable students to become comfortable enough with the skill to complete it in a distracting environment. These are the decisions of the instructional designer, but these decisions are much easier to make when the objective is specific. When an instructional designer is clear on the conditions under which the student must perform and the level to which the student needs to perform, it is easier for the designer to create a program that enables achievement of the goal. The conditions on the job and the skill level needed are paramount to ensuring the proper rigor in the instructional strategy and in the mastery by the student. Only by considering the job conditions and skill requirements can the instructional designer hope to design a program that leads to behavior change on the job and influences the metric that measures the behavior change.

How Measurable Instructional Design™ Impacts Training Evaluation

The components of Measurable Instructional Design™ enable a training program to be measured and evaluated. By connecting the business metric to behaviors that impact the metric, and then creating measurable objectives that are linked to instructional strategies and evaluation methods, we can see a direct link between the intent of instruction and the achievement of the program goals. More specifically, the key to being able to evaluate training and show training impact is in designing a program using the best practices of instructional design.

In design, measuring impact requires being specific about what change needs to be made, clear on the improvements to performance necessary to achieve the change, and evaluating results against the required changes to performance. Instead of trying to show value by highlighting the number of courses produced or survey results that show the perception of impact, specific instructional design allows you to create a direct connection between the objectives of a course and the mastery. This produces certainty in impact.

The development of e-learning and the use of new technology in training have required us to adapt instructional methods to fit these new mediums. Due to this trend, we have focused on learning the latest technology and improving our instructional delivery methods instead of focusing on the competency needed to ensure our design results. If we cannot show how our programs impact business results through knowledge and skill gains that improve performance, then we cannot demonstrate our real value to stakeholders. New technologies that enable cool instructional methods like video and gaming hold little value if they do not enable students to perform better on the job. If we as instructional designers do not show our ability to apply adult learning theory and performance improvement knowledge to our design, then our value will only be as high as the newest or coolest tool that we are able to use.

Measureable Instructional Design™ enables training professionals to **clearly demonstrate how their training design creates the behavior changes that can impact performance**. Measureable Instructional Design™ also allows training professionals to achieve predictable results because it tests the impact against a specific design. Specificity in design greatly reduces variation in training results. The more we measure our success, the more we will learn about the best ways to analyze performance gaps and fill those gaps with effective instructional strategies.

Most importantly, Measureable Instructional Design™ allows training professionals to truly see their impact on an organization. If we begin to understand the influence that design has on results, we learn what training can (and cannot) do. Once we become clear on how we make an impact, we can focus on delivering training that will improve business results and begin supporting our organization in other ways when training is not the answer.

Measurable Instructional Design™ in Review

In Part I of this book, Analysis, we looked at how the analysis stage of instructional design is paramount in ensuring that training results reflect the needs of the organization. In Part II, Design, we outlined the critical parts of design that enable training to be quantified and laid the foundation for creating the chain of evidence needed to show impact. These two parts make up Measurable Instructional Design™ (MID). The MID process incorporates the best practices in instructional design to support the instructional designer in the development of impactful and measurable training. Over the years, our company has certified many organizations (and independent instructional designers) on the MID methodology. The clarity provided by using the model has been powerful in opening the conversation between instructional designers and business managers. In addition, instructional designers using the model have graciously shared their stories about their own growth in understanding their value. This is the most important thing for me, as I am certain once instructional designers are clear on the value of their design, the training industry will gain the means to really impact the direction of a company. The foundational components of the MID process have been provided in the preceding chapters to show the logical progression in the chain of evidence needed to show training's impact. The intention was not to "teach" the model, only to inform of the basic components. Some details in the steps were provided to support understanding of how the chain of evidence is created.

The MID process is a component of the ROI by Design™ model. Using the MID process enables you to have a training program that focuses on a business KPM, addresses a business learning goal, ensures objectives are targeted to performance, and confirms that mastery is directly linked to the objectives. The next two parts of the book focus on the evaluation of the MID training program and identification of the results gained.

Case Study – The Select Group – The Design

Once the standards were determined, eParamus™ designed a course that matched the skills used in the recruiter role. The Select Group wanted the training to be more challenging than the recruiting process itself so new recruiters would be prepared to handle any scenario they encountered on the job.

The Select Group brings in the new recruiter hires for an instructor-led two-week training session. As a part of the training, the new recruiters are provided the standards of performance. The course objectives reflected the specific conditions of the job and included the level of performance indicated in the standards. Metrics used to measure the success of the recruiter role were used to determine the goal and specific objectives to address. Objectives were vastly weighted toward skills to ensure a high comfort level as new recruiters transferred from the classroom to the job. Instructional strategies were reflective of the actual work environment whenever possible and allowed for significant practice of the required skills.

The mastery exam was directly linked to the objectives. For every skill objective, skills practice was included as part of the instructional strategy and corresponding mastery was based on the standards of performance of the skill. These essential evaluation steps will be discussed in Chapter 3, Evaluation.

3

EVALUATION

Incorporating business focus into the analysis and design of training helps create courses that are measureable and ensures the ability to evaluate outcomes (or results). It is much easier to evaluate training programs when they are designed to consider the behavior changes needed to have an impact on the organization.

As mentioned in the introduction to this book, in 1959, Donald Kirkpatrick theorized about the four levels of training evaluation.

- The first level is **Reaction**. This level evaluates how the student reacted to the training. Did he or she like it? What did the student think of the training? How did the student feel about the training process?
- The second level is **Learning**. What did the student learn in the training? Did the student attain new knowledge or skills?

- The third level is **Behavior**. Did the student transfer the knowledge from the classroom to the job? Did the student's behavior change because of the training?
- The fourth level is **Results**. How did the training and resultant behavior change impact the organization? What were the tangible, measurable results of the training to the company?

We will refer to these levels as we discuss evaluation levels and models.

Differences in Evaluation Models

Based on current research, we know the measurement of training is limited. But when training is measured, what models are being used to evaluate the training? We know the most frequent type of measurement is at level one (92% of organizations complete this type of measurement). As mentioned above, level one measures the student's reaction to training and typically consists of a questionnaire that asks students how they felt about the training. Administered at the end of class, either in class or through an online survey, the questionnaire often asks about the skill of the facilitator, the relevance of the objectives, if the training objectives were met, and if the student believed he or she would use the material gained from the training program.

The second level of evaluation—learning—is measured less often and is typically determined via a test of what the student learned during the course. Most often the test is a series of multiple choice or true/false questions that address topics covered in class and focus on the student's grasp of the content.

Finally, levels three and four (behavior change and results) are rarely measured. If they are measured, it is usually done by a questionnaire that asks students how much they think the training will be used on the job and how much they think the organization will be impacted by the training.

Evaluation methods can be categorized into two major types—perception models and impact models. Understanding the difference is crucial for deciding which type to use.

Perception Models

Companies often use their learning management system (LMS) to administer knowledge tests or surveys to determine the impact of their training. Levels one, three, and four are often measured by surveys. Therefore, the preponderance of evidence regarding training impact on the learner and the organization boils down to perception. Even when a company uses a knowledge test to determine what a student learned in class, that test is often followed by a survey to determine if the knowledge they gained was applicable to their jobs, if they used the knowledge, and if the organization benefited from the training.

When we think of surveys, we think of using them to glean information about someone's view or opinion. Surveys are used in marketing research, opinion polls, TV or radio ratings, or anywhere there is a need to get a general idea of how someone feels about something. When you use a survey to assess training what do you get? A general idea of how they feel about the training. You get students who tell you if they *think* the content was relevant, if they *think* they will use the content on the job, and if they *think* using that content will actually make a change to the organization. You get their perception (opinion) of impact! Perception models essentially treat the training design as a "black box" because they do not address results in relation to the acquisition of knowledge and skills provided in the course content. If the opinions were negative, there is no way to know if the student actually learned the content or how to repair the issue because opinions are not tied to actual performance. Perception models measure opinion as opposed to measurement of intended results.

How much can you count on survey results (that only indicate a student's opinion) to determine impact? In your own organization, have you witnessed survey results that said the students thought the training was relevant, thought it would be used, and thought it would have an impact, even though there was no discernible change in behavior? Most would agree that what people *think* they will do, what they *say* they will do, and what they *actually do* can be very different things.

Impact Models

Instead of relying on opinions produced by using a perception (survey) model, training results can be measured using an impact model. This type of model evaluates by measuring actual business results, or impact. ROI by Design™ is an impact model.

To measure impact for training, you must first consider what the actual impact of training should be. The goal of any training program is centered on creating a behavior change. Unlike education, which seeks to provide a broad understanding of concepts, training is focused on creating a behavior change within an organization. Training in organizations supports the development of a specific set of behavior changes and competencies necessary to move an organization forward. Therefore, training impact can be measured by the actual behavior change addressed by the training program.

As discussed in the Analysis chapter, to design a training program, you must first determine the new behaviors needed and the key performance metrics that will measure the behavior change. Since training can only impact knowledge, skills, or attitudes, you should only create a training program when a gain in a knowledge or skill is needed to create behavior change. When training is produced that does not address a clear gap in knowledge or skill, there is no clear way to determine if the goal is achieved. A training course that does not contribute to either knowledge or skill gain may be interesting to the learner, but will not create a behavior change or have a clear impact on the organization.

The impact model of measurement does not rely on student perception. Rather it measures knowledge and skill gain by directly testing for it. The ROI by Design™ impact model measures knowledge and skill before the training and compares it to a measure immediately after the training, and then again several months after the training. In addition, it measures the intended organizational impact (the key performance metric [KPM]) before and after the training to confirm that the behavior changes actually impacted the identified metric.

The Comparison of Evaluation Models table on the next page provides an overview of impact and perception models and the difference in results at the various measurement stages.

Comparison of Evaluation Models

BUSINESS IMPACT 2.0® METHODOLOGY — IMPACT MODEL				
JOB/SKILL ANALYSIS • ESTABLISH LEARNING KPM	COURSE DESIGN FACILITATION	QUANTIFIED JOB KNOWLEDGE/ SKILL CAPABILITY	QUANTIFIED JOB KNOWLEDGE/ SKILL RETENTION • JOB APPLICATION	KPM/COMPANY METRIC • TREND ANALYSIS
OTHER ROI METHODOLOGIES — PERCEPTION MODEL				
PERCEPTION OF NEED	BLACK BOX	PERCEPTION OF TRAINING RESULTS	PERCEPTION OF CHANGE	PERCEPTION OF FUTURE IMPACT • BEFORE/AFTER METRIC REVIEW
TRAINING NEED	TRAINING PRODUCT	CLASSROOM RESULTS	JOB TRANSFER RESULTS	COMPANY IMPACT

← PROJECT PHASES →

An impact model clarifies what has been gained from a training program. Those results can be provided to all stakeholders as evidence of the real value of the training program. Unlike perception models, impact models provide empirical evidence of knowledge and skill gains, and direct evidence of how the behavior changes derived from training benefitted the organization.

Basic Evaluation Points

Evaluating programs at specific impact points allows training results to be visible and allows problems with lack of learning, retention, and application to be addressed. There are specific points in the evaluation process where measurement shows a clear picture of the impact of training at a particular phase. By measuring at each point you can repair any issues related to impact before moving on to the next point. The points in training evaluation include:

- Baseline KPM
- Pre-assessment
- Post-test
- Transfer test
- Post KPM

These evaluation points show the progression of impact. Depending upon what you learn at each point, you may or may not move forward with measurement of the next point. If there is no growth in the student between the pre-assessment and the post-test then you would not expect transfer of knowledge or skill to the job. You can recognize that there is a problem between the pre-assessment and post-test and address/resolve that first before continuing the program.

Intervention Opportunities

Each evaluation point provides information on the process and consequently provides an intervention opportunity. The first two points—baseline KPM and pre-assessment—provide a baseline measurement for the organization and the individual. The baseline KPM helps to identify the level currently achieved by the organization. The pre-assessment helps to identify the current level of knowledge or skill the student has and the gap between the current level and what is needed.

The post-test and transfer test indicate how well students learned in the classroom and how well they retained the knowledge or skill after training. In addition, the post KPM compared to the baseline KPM shows the change in the metric due to the training program.

Furthermore, comparing different points provides valuable information on the progress made due to the training program. A summary of the comparisons of the impact points and what they tell you is below:

- The **pre-assessment** compared to the **post-test** shows the amount of knowledge and skill gain achieved in the classroom.
- The **post-test** compared to the **transfer test** shows the amount of knowledge and skill gain that the student retained and used in the organization.
- The **baseline KPM** compared to the **post KPM** shows the amount of change in the KPM due to the training program.

The comparisons between the pre-assessment, post-test, and transfer test show the changes in the students due to the training program. The comparison of the baseline KPM and the post KPM shows the changes in the organization that resulted from the behavior changes influenced by the training program.

When you consider Kirkpatrick's levels and the comparison of impact points you can easily see where they align. The following shows the comparisons and their correlations to Kirkpatrick level:

- The **pre-assessment** compared to the **post-test** correlates to Kirkpatrick level two—learning.
- The **post-test** compared to the **transfer test** correlates to Kirkpatrick level three—behavior.
- The **baseline KPM** compared to the **post KPM** correlates to Kirkpatrick level four—results.

Kirkpatrick's model provides a good framework for showing where training can impact an organization, but it stops short of describing the methods used for measurement. ***The ROI by Design™ evaluation model uses the best practices in training design to provide the means to measure at the identified levels.***

Levels of Evaluation

Each individual evaluation point in the ROI by Design™ model provides valuable information. Some points provide information on the need for training in the organization, some provide information on the student's need for training, and still others provide information on the status of acquisition of learning or the application of learning. Each point by itself provides good information on the status of learning at a single point in time. In addition to the information provided by each evaluation point individually, the comparison between two evaluation points provides the information on the progress of the program.

Progress of a training program can be measured both at the individual level and the classroom level. The measurement at the individual level provides information on the progression of individual students. The measurement at the classroom level provides information on the training process and its impact on the group. Classroom-level measures show the effectiveness of the training program and the ability of the organization to support the retention and application of the newly gained knowledge and skills.

Level Two Evaluation and Intervention Opportunities

A level two evaluation is an evaluation of the learning. Organizations use pre-tests and post-tests to see the growth in learning due to the course. Typically organizations have only measured the pre and post at the individual level. However, by measuring at both the individual and classroom levels, the training professional can determine the interventions necessary to support both the student's growth and the organization's growth. Let's consider the level two impact points, which are the pre-assessment and post-test. The typical expectation is that each student's pre-assessment scores would be low and post-test scores would be higher.

What do you do if your expectations are confounded, such as a high pre-assessment score or a low post-test score? A high pre-assessment at the individual level and the class level tells you something different. If there is a high pre-assessment from an individual student you know that the student already has a high level of knowledge or skill in the training content. You then have the opportunity to decide if that student really needs to take time away from his or her job to take the course.

However, if you have a high pre-assessment at the classroom level (class average) then you would know that most of the class already has the knowledge or skill covered in the course. You then have the opportunity to assess if the course is needed at all. If most students can pass the test before you administer the course, then why run the course? A high pre-assessment at the classroom level also prompts you to ask the obvious question: What part of your analysis was wrong? If your analysis determined the need for the course but the students the course was intended for already have the knowledge and skill, then your determination of the need for the training was faulty.

When a high pre-assessment is present, you have several intervention methods to choose from. You can choose to exempt high pre-assessment students from the course, redesign the course to increase rigor, or end the project. If there is a high pre-assessment and no action is taken, then you can expect a lack of student engagement, a higher potential for drop out, low (if any) probability of job impact, and student dissatisfaction with the course.

The second impact point for level two is the post-test. At level two you want a high post-test score, which would indicate an effective learning experience. A low class average or low individual post-test score indicates learning did not take place. If an individual student has a low post-test (but the class average was high), then you can conclude that the individual student has a competency issue. You need to decide how to support the student in gaining the necessary knowledge and skill. Your options may include having the student repeat the course or providing the student with a mentor to help him or her gain the skills. There are several ways to address the challenge, but the point is that when you evaluate the individual student at this impact point you are able to intervene and support the student.

When there is a low post-test at the classroom level, you learn something different. If the classroom average reflects a low post-test then you know that the course was not effective. If you compare the pre-assessment average to the post-test average you will learn exactly how ineffective the course was at achieving the objectives. A course can be ineffective due to poor course design or poor course facilitation. By comparing the pre-assessment and the post-test average, a very clear picture of the areas of poor design or facilitation can be found.

The evaluation at the individual level and classroom level as well as the comparison of the pre-assessment and post-test points is important for training success. When there is a low post-test result at the classroom level and no action is taken, there is a low probability of job impact, manager dissatisfaction with course results, and student dissatisfaction with the course.

If there is a low post-test present at the classroom level and a comparison of the pre-assessment and post-test shows poor performance across the class, you can then either repeat the course with new or improved design or repeat the course with a new or improved facilitator to ensure effectiveness and impact in the organization.

Level Three Evaluation and Intervention Opportunities

The level three measurement measures the retention and application of knowledge or skills. This is known as transfer. You measure transfer by comparing the participant's performance on the post-test to their performance after they have returned to the job.

Level three evaluation tests many things including:

- Individual retention and application of knowledge and skills
- How well the training content aligned with the job function
- The extent of the manager's support of training
- Environmental factors that inhibit use of newly developed knowledge or skills

The level three evaluations are made by looking at the transfer test score at both the individual level and the classroom level. Looking at an individual student's transfer score indicates how well the student retained the training information and how well the student applied the learning to the job. If the classroom measurement of transfer showed most people in the class were able to retain and apply the knowledge and skills, then a poor individual score indicates poor performance in the individual. Once this is realized, steps to support the individual student can be taken.

By comparing the class average post-test and the class average transfer test you can assess the transfer process and identify how well the organizational environment supported or inhibited transfer. If the class post-test scores were good then you know that the training intervention was successful. If after a successful training intervention the average class transfer test score was poor, then you recognize training was successful but there is an environmental factor that inhibits the students from applying the new knowledge and skills. Without application of new knowledge and skills, the newly acquired capabilities are lost. Measuring for transfer is a very important step to ensure the ability of a training program to impact an organization. Acquiring knowledge and skills is an essential part of the process, but without application, the organization will not see any real impact from the time and money spent on training.

When low transfer is present and no action is taken, the training program is often incorrectly viewed as ineffective, job performance is not impacted, students become dissatisfied with training, and the identified KPM is not impacted. The lack of measuring transfer has done a lot to damage the reputation of training.

When using an impact model, which measures for behavior changes, the factors that inhibit transfer become very clear. Testing for behavior change allows clarity. If students acquired the behaviors in the classroom (determined by comparing the pre-assessment and post tests) and then do not apply those behaviors and therefore do not pass at transfer (determined by comparing the post-test to the transfer test) attention can be given to looking at factors outside of the training program that inhibit training application and success. Over the years, many of our clients have discovered several things within their organizations—such as processes, systems, competing policy, or lack of management support—that unknowingly impaired the training impact.

Level Four Evaluation and Intervention Opportunities

Both levels two and three measure behavior changes in students. Level four measures if the behavior change equated to organizational change.

The health of an organization is typically measured by capturing and reviewing metrics. In an organization, metrics show the outputs from people, processes, and systems within the organization. In measurable training, it is necessary to identify which metrics are impacted by human performance and then measure those metrics before and after the training to show training's impact to an organization.

If level three does not indicate a change in behavior, then an organizational metric would not be impacted. Therefore, level four is only measured when level three is effective. Only if knowledge/skill transfer took place and that knowledge/skill was applied on the job can level four be measured. If you do not see an actual behavior change take place on the job, then you cannot expect for the measured outputs in the organization to change. Unlike the other levels, level four is not measured at the individual level because level four is intended only to measure changes to the company. Changes to the company only come when there is a collective behavior change.

If you research level four metrics in training you will find that the challenge has centered on isolation of the variable to measure. Unfortunately, this means most training professionals have spent their time either working on ways to isolate the impact of training against everything else that may have impacted the metric, or they spend their time explaining why level four is not important because it cannot be isolated.

The MID process provides another option for measuring level four, the foundation of which is determining the correct metric at the analysis stage. As outlined in the Analysis section, but still bears repeating now, many training professionals try to tie training impact to strategic metrics instead of operational metrics. Most young organizations begin determining the health of their organization by developing strategic metrics, which are high-level measures used to determine the overall health of an organization. As they grow and mature, organizations begin to develop more operational metrics to measure their business. Operational metrics are more targeted than strategic metrics and often measure how well people perform a task or series of tasks or how well a process works. An example of an operational metric would be employee X produces Y number of widgets in Z number of hours. An operational metric may measure exactly how many widgets are produced per hour (by shift). On the other hand, a strategic metric may measure the profit on the widget. To measure the profit you must consider the number of widgets produced in the hour but you must also consider the cost of the raw materials, the competitor's price, and the skill of the sales personnel! With the many different factors that impact a strategic metric, it is very difficult to isolate the impact of a performance on the result.

With strategic metrics there are several things that impact results, such as people, processes, and systems within the organization. On the other hand, operational metrics are more targeted and often measure how well people perform a task or series of tasks or how well a process works. Operational metrics are very common in the manufacturing environment. If you have ever seen a manufacturing environment you will notice they have measurements for almost every area of production. Since manufacturing companies make money based on how much, how well, and how efficiently they produce an item, they get very good at measuring steps in their process and results from performance on a task.

Manufacturing is an easy example to consider, but in fact, all organizations use operational metrics of some type all the time. For example, recruiting firms measure how many candidates their recruiters qualify or how well the candidates are qualified for the positions. These are operational metrics that can be directly tied to performance (behavior). In another example, a drug safety company measures how accurately or quickly a case manager completes a case. A marketing communications company may measure how well a manager develops his or her employees. There are certain behaviors that lead to results in an organization and are captured in operational metrics. Determining those operational metrics is the key to determining training's impact on an organization.

In training analysis, an investigation of a gap in performance is made. If you are able to determine how the organization knows there is a training need, you often find the metric that measures the behavior. As discussed in the Analysis chapter, department managers have several indicators they watch to see if their department is performing well. These indicators are measurements they make on a regular basis and often become the KPM for training because they help the manager identify the problem with performance.

Level four evaluation comes from the measurement of the baseline KPM (before the training) compared to the post KPM (after transfer is successful). Dependent on the size of the class in the training program, you may find the need to measure the operational metric at the department level or the enterprise level. If training is intended for a manager or a leader, the metric may be something that reflects the results of the newly acquired behavior. At the manager level, you may measure a KPM showing the behavior of their direct reports. For example, if you have manager training that teaches a manager to be responsive to employee suggestions, you might use the number of ideas submitted in the suggestion box as one of your metrics. Or if you have training that teaches managers the skills necessary to communicate business goals and objectives well to their employees, then your metric may be employee awareness of business objectives.

The main objective is to identify the metric that you believe will be the best measurement of impact based on the need and the content of training. You may find that several metrics are influenced by a behavior change. As you begin to identify these operational metrics and measure them against the change in behavior created in training, you will be able to create a good list of the training programs that truly impact the metric. If transfer is successful, but the metric you identified is not impacted, then it is important to determine if any other metric was impacted by the training intervention. The bottom line process is this:

- Look closely at what metrics uncovered the problem.
- Test those same metrics for changes after the training transfer is successful.
- Look for any other metrics that may have changed.

These three steps make you successful at determining which metrics are impacted by performance and which behaviors impact that performance.

Financial ROI

In addition to identifying metric changes due to training, another way to show value is determining financial ROI. Financial ROI can be calculated by capturing the costs of training and translating the percentage change in the operational metric to a numerical value. This calculation can easily be made if you track costs and measure metric changes.

It has been my experience that many organizations do not translate their metrics to financial terms at this level. Understanding what impacts a metric seems to be enough for most organizations. However, it is important to note that with the ROI by Design™ evaluation model you can determine financial results. Business Impact 2.0 software helps our customers design measurable training, evaluate their programs, and capture their costs. If metrics in an organization are translated into financial terms, then the software will also make the ROI calculation for them.

Accountability for Training Results

Looking at the different levels of evaluation and the different impact points, you begin to clearly see how training results are dependent on several stakeholders. Determining the right programs to run, designing the programs well, and supporting the learning on the job requires training requesters, training professionals, and business managers to work together. Each stakeholder is responsible for success and is therefore accountable. The ROI by Design™ Model Accountability Diagram shows accountability across the training continuum.

ROI by Design Model Accountability Diagram

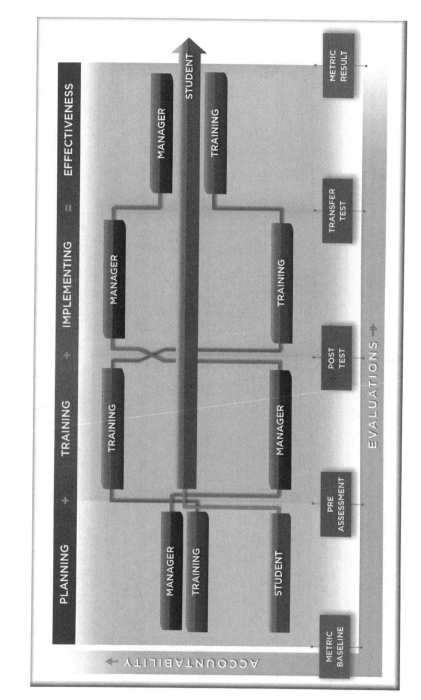

The diagram shows that in the planning stages, the manager (or training requester) and the trainer share accountability for planning the training program. Clear communication regarding what training is needed (the gap), what to include in the training, and how to measure the success of training is necessary for the program to be successful. This information can only be complete when there is collaboration between the business manager (requester) and trainer stakeholders. During this stage the KPM and standards of performance are determined. Training delivery follows the planning stages. The trainer has the highest accountability during the training stage because he or she has the most influence over the design and facilitation of the program.

Once the training program has been successfully delivered, the learning implementation stage begins. The manager has the most accountability during this stage because he or she has the greatest influence over the student's environment and is the stakeholder that has the ability to support the transfer of the skills.

Using the ROI by Design™ model, you can review impact points along the evaluation stages. In addition, you can isolate accountability, which enables you to easily determine problems with impact and intervene with solutions should any issues arise. Evaluating at specific impact points provides the credible evidence of the point of failure. This evidence enables transparency on the possible reasons for failure. By isolating the point of failure, the options for repair are targeted to those who have the accountability for success at the failure stage. In addition, the model reflects a logical progression, so transfer is not expected if knowledge and skills are not gained in training, and impact is not expected if transfer has not been achieved. This information helps you to be proactive in supplying interventions and prescriptive in the expected results.

Case Study – The Select Group – Evaluation

Before deploying the new recruiter training, a pre-assessment of the training group was completed. The testing and measurement was accomplished with Business Impact 2.0, a proprietary tool created by eParamus™. The initial testing established a baseline for each trainee. The pre-assessment also enabled trainees the opportunity to see the breadth of the program and understand the performance level they were expected to achieve during the training as well as later on the job.

The program itself includes reading, review, and discussion. However, a key component is role-playing sessions. During the first week of the session, trainees role-play steps from the recruiting process with senior leaders and trainers. After these sessions, they receive immediate feedback. In the second week, trainees put their new skills into action. Again, they receive immediate feedback. At the end of the two-week session, a post-test establishes the rate of knowledge and skill transfer. Based on the post-test results, the course facilitator develops objectives for trainees to achieve in their first six weeks on the job.

At the end of the six weeks, a transfer test is administered. The test results show how well recruiters are executing in the field compared to how they performed at the end of the course.

The level 4 metric baselines were established by reviewing the productivity of recruiters prior to the implementation of the new recruiter onboarding course. The baseline prior to training was compared to the productivity metrics after transfer of the new recruiter training.

In addition to using the measurements as a means to determine the effectiveness of the training, The Select Group was able to use the assessment created for the recruiter training as a means to assess the competency levels of their new hires as well as recruiters who have been on the job for years. This practice enabled TSG to ensure best practices were consistently followed across the organization.

RESULTS

The bottom line for any new process or procedure is what results can be seen from its implementation. Let's consider what results can be derived from using the MID best practices and following the ROI by Design™ impact model. There are two major areas where results can be seen with the application of the model. Major results will be realized by both the organization and the training industry.

Results for the Organization

The biggest unanswered question that organizations have with regard to training is what outcomes and value do we get from the thousands of dollars spent on it each year. Training professionals need to logically show how training creates value by developing employees and preparing them to meet the challenges in the organization. By incorporating the instructional design best practices described in this book and using an impact evaluation model, you can show important changes in both **employee behavior** and **key performance metrics** that are affected by behavior changes. In addition, you can create actionable and **repeatable** training that can directly link results achieved to dollars spent. Furthermore, when using the ROI by Design™ methodology, you will see **increased collaboration** between the training function and the business unit managers.

Identification of Important Behaviors

Let's first consider the power of identifying important organizational behaviors. The high cost of employee development is mainly due to the understanding that the right knowledge and skills lead to the right competencies and critical behaviors needed within an organization. Highly competent people provide an important competitive advantage for a business. In addition to advanced technologies and products used by an organization, the people in an organization are the main determinants of success. By using the best instructional design practices outlined in the ROI by Design™ model, you can identify the important behaviors that lead to success. Identifying these behaviors and cultivating them within your organization allows you to gain the competitive advantage of a highly competent workforce.

Key behaviors have always been the expected outcomes from training programs. Even programs that are centered on knowledge focus on using that knowledge to change behavior. Organizations invest in training to improve their people. That improvement is reflected in individual behavior. Metrics measure the collective results of individual behavior and the systems and processes within an organization. The ROI by Design™ methodology enables behaviors to be identified, quantified, and achieved. It is this specificity that allows you to show the value of training.

If you design programs with specific organizational goals and create objectives with clear conditions and criteria for success, you can quantify the behaviors that are most impactful to your organizational success. The very specific goals created by using the ROI by Design™ model permit actionable and repeatable outcomes from training. This means repeatable behavior changes!

Behavior's Impact on Key Operational Metrics

When important organizational behaviors are identified, it becomes easier to discover key performance metrics that are impacted by training. In current training literature, there are many references regarding the identification of metrics, but very few address how to apply them. Theory with little application is usually a sign that people are making something too difficult. Instead of trying to take metrics that are influenced by several things fit the training outputs, the ROI by Design™ model works to identify the direct causal metrics first and monitors any correlating metrics. This identification means an organization can categorize the exact measures that will show training success, as well as the behaviors that impact the metric. The methodology uses focused and specific design to create a chain of evidence to show the connection between the organizational metric and the training design element that can achieve a behavior change and influence the metric.

After continuous use of the model, an organization begins to build a substantial metric hierarchy. This hierarchy shows all of the operational metrics associated with training and all of the strategic metrics that correlate. In other words, the organization creates a concrete means of seeing the metrics that indicate the results of a behavior change. This helps an organization isolate these metrics from others that are not influenced by training. In addition, it helps an organization to proactively cultivate metrics that reflect performance. The better organizations understand what influences their performance metrics, the better they are able to improve them!

Repeatable Outcomes

Another major result from the use of this methodology in an organization is the ability to ensure consistent repeatable outcomes from training. In much of traditional training design, objectives and measurements can be ambiguous. This ambiguity often creates a different learning outcome dependent on the facilitator's personality and the interpretation of the design elements. On the other hand, ROI by Design™ drives instructional design that is measurable and completed in such a way as to outline clear and specific objectives and a clear and specific means of measurement. This effective instructional design standardizes design elements so that every time the training is completed, it is completed in the same way.

The MID standardization ensures the identification of a metric that is associated to behavior standards. It directly links the metrics, behaviors, objectives, and measurement throughout the design. It ensures the instructional strategies that are chosen achieve the conditions and criteria of the standards of performance. This standardization of effective design allows for repeatable results.

The ROI by Design™ method also ensures repeatable outcomes by alerting the organization to failures in the process via skill measurement at various impact points in learner development. If expected results are not achieved at these points of impact, the organization has the opportunity to intervene and repair the problem. This allows the organization to be consistently aware of results and empowers them to consistently repair issues when needed. By closing the loop on expected results and alerting an organization if the results are not achieved at each stage, a strong learning organization is created and the real value of training is realized.

Increased Organizational Collaboration

A vital component of any organization is good communication. One of the significant challenges facing trainers in an organization is collaborating with the business unit managers, who are typically the customers of the training department. The challenge mainly comes from a difference in focus and language between the training department and the other departments in an organization. Training departments focus on the development of people in the organization and talk in terms of learning. Other departments focus on business outputs and talk in terms of productivity. The ROI by Design™ model teaches instructional designers how to align their efforts with the business goals, how to connect learning goals to business goals, and how to **communicate** about the training program using business terms.

In addition to collaborating with the organizational managers on training goals, objectives, outputs, and measurements along the training continuum, there is increased collaboration within the organization on how the student progresses from the classroom to the job. In the ROI by Design™ model, measurements are made on both the learning by the individual and the learning process. By measuring at specific impact points, accountability for training results at each stage becomes clearly visible. Clarity around who has the ability to impact learning and the transfer of learning enables productive dialog and a means to improve the success of both.

In summary, increased collaboration will improve communication allowing for training to focus on business goals, leading more often to the expected results, and removing barriers to the transfer of skills.

Results for the Training Profession

The outcomes achieved from using the ROI by Design™ methodology justify the efforts to learn the process and support the implementation of the best practices it employs. Organizations will certainly benefit from ROI by Design™ but it's the training industry that will realize the greatest gain from using this new methodology.

When the ROI by Design™ model is used, the training profession can expect a greater identification of training's value, clarity of training roles, and a greater ability to secure training budgets.

Identification of Training's Value

The identity crisis in the training profession is largely due to an inability to clearly show how training efforts impact organizational outcomes. Using the ROI by Design™ methodology connects the learning processes to the business process and permits measurement against business gains. The ROI by Design™ model creates transparency and clarity in how training efforts support the organizational goals.

The use of surveys as the main means to show training impact has served to position training as something that cannot be quantified. The inability to quantify impact has set training apart from other departments and contributed to the notion that training is a cost center instead of a function that enables productivity. With the ROI by Design™ methodology, the training department can demonstrate its value when learners acquire skills (behaviors) that are necessary to effectively run a business and metrics to show the results of the behaviors. This new ability is huge for identifying and quantifying the value of training.

In the past, executives may have *felt* that training added value and so they used training when and where they could. However, they would cut training investment or even eliminate training budgets when money became tight because they have been unable to quantify its value. The ROI by Design™ model enables you to quantify (not just *feel* or *perceive*, but actually *quantify*) training results, which demonstrates real repeatable value!

Clarity of the Training Role

Over the past several years, I have had the benefit of attending professional organization conferences such as those held by the American Society for Training and Development (ASTD), the Academy of Human Resource Development (AHRD), and the International Society for Performance Improvement (ISPI). At these conferences, there have been lively discussions regarding the training role and the competencies necessary for that role. It is hard to believe that the profession meant to help develop skills and competencies in the workforce struggles with how to best do this for itself.

I often ask groups of trainers the following questions:

- What is your value to an organization?
- What is training's product?
- What is the value of training to your customer?

When answering those questions, it becomes evident that the **value of the training role is centered on the ability to design, develop, and implement training programs that improve**

organizational productivity. If our value is in this ability, and we can measure the impact of training activities in business terms, then clarity of the training role becomes obvious.

As discussed in the introduction, lack of clarity in the training role can lead to devaluing the role. Often trainers will identify their role as a supporter role that helps others attain competency. When trainers identify their primary role as that of a mentor, coach, regulator, etc., the question becomes how a supporter role helps to deliver the expected training results. What value do supporter activities provide in achieving the training product?

Certainly, there are companies that expect trainers to play a supporting or mentoring role to employees as part of their job, but when compared to what the training department is expected to produce, it is difficult to accept the supporter role as primary. The trainer's competency to design, develop, and deliver an adult learning program that changes behavior in a measurable way makes his or her function clear to the organization and establishes expertise.

Establishing an area of expertise is important. For instance, when a trainer has an established area of expertise in designing courses and recommends a certain time frame for establishing a skill or a certain instructional strategy to accomplish a skill, the customer (business manager) is likely to defer to the trainer in how to accomplish the goal. On the other hand, when the role and expertise of the trainer are misunderstood or understated, the business manager may allow the trainer to produce the program, but will put conditions on the trainer, such as the time frame to run the program or a particular method of teaching because they do not recognize the trainer's area of expertise in making these decisions.

The lack of clarity occurs when trainers focus on things outside of their areas of expertise. If their area of expertise is ambiguous, it becomes very difficult to show their proficiency. If a trainer describes herself as a mentor or a coach in the training role, how does that make her different from a professional coach or organizational psychologist? Is the trainer's background in education, adult learning, and instructional design or is it in coaching and psychology? Being clear about your role and expertise lends credibility to your outputs.

Sometimes trainers describe themselves as content experts and therefore assume they can conduct training in their particular content area. When this happens, they dismiss the expertise of designing a learning event in favor of being a subject matter expert who trains. This would imply that there is no skill or expertise needed to design a program, but only subject knowledge. If training requesters do not understand the skill set required to be a good instructional designer, then it is difficult to expect them to defer to the trainer in the design.

In brief, by using the ROI by Design™ model, you make your training role clear and you measure against your ability to design and facilitate an effective program. Your ability to design, facilitate, and measure a training program is demonstrated by identifying specific points that measure success. When you measure both the training program and the training process, you can isolate the impact at the classroom stage and the transfer stage. You can show the learner's progress and the organizational progress directly tied to training design efforts. This ability highlights the trainer's impact and clarifies his or her role. Being able to show this effectiveness illuminates your expertise in developing an organization and defines your role!

Securing Training Budgets

Perhaps the ultimate benefit of using the ROI by Design™ methodology is the ability to secure your training budget. If there is one thing most training professionals can agree on, it is that securing the training budget is a challenge. At budget time, organizational leaders often consider training a "nice to have" instead of a "need to have" expense, making it easy to cut. If you have no way to measure your impact on the organization or demonstrate your expertise, you may find it harder to defend the training portion of the budget.

Most organizations have a limited budget and must consider all of the needs of departments when making allocations. Organizations find certain things necessary for their business to run. Those things may include software systems, unfinished goods to produce a product, or fixed expenses such as facility costs and salaries. Those things are secured in the budget first because they provide the operational foundation of the business.

Once the foundational money is allocated, the remaining (discretionary) budget can be distributed. Discretionary spending is often based on value. What money spent will deliver the most value? If you cannot clearly articulate the value of training, you may find your training budget decrease. The training department budget often receives the most scrutiny and seems easier to dispense with because the effects of reducing training are not immediately seen.

Use of the ROI by Design™ model provides clear evidence of behaviors that have changed and metrics that have been impacted due to training efforts. With consistent use of the ROI by Design™ model, a trainer can easily provide predictability of impact and supply the credible evidence needed to secure the training budget. Once the ROI by Design™ methodology is used, results can be captured and highlighted. Once the results are known, senior executives have an easier time understanding the value of training and can quantify what will happen with the reduction of training.

Business is always about results. The ROI by Design™ methodology provides the results organizations look for from training. The ROI by Design™ methodology assists the training profession in showing their true value and, in turn, helps secure the budgets necessary to allow training professionals to keep improving employee performance!

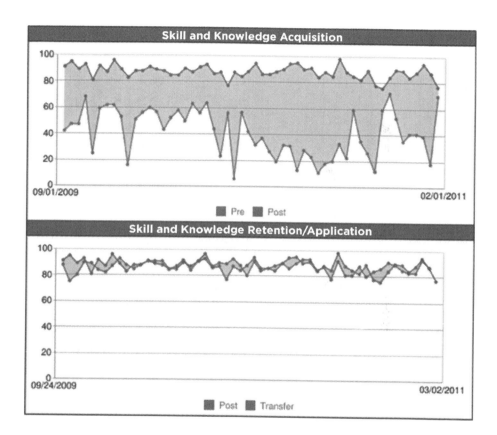

These graphs indicate the level of student learning. "Skill and Knowledge Acquisition" shows learning acquired during training. "Skill and Knowledge Retention/Application" shows the transfer of learning from the classroom to the job.

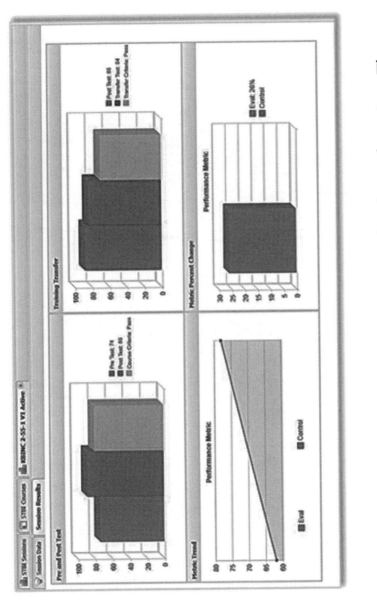

These graphs show a series of courses and indicate learning. They include acquisition of learning during training, retention of learning after return to the job, and impact on the business metrics targeted by the program.

Case Study – The Select Group – Results

The high level of application to the job in the recruiter training course enabled The Select Group to have trainees who made beneficial phone calls in their second week of training. There were also some trainees who had offers accepted within their first week on the job after they completed the course. This provided immediate revenue to the organization.

Development of standards for each skill, as well as measurement of success of the skill within the training and on the job, enabled The Select Group to make modifications to standards in order to increase the efficiency of the skills.

Reports from the Business Impact 2.0 system created a dialog between the training department and the floor managers and helped align management with the training process. It also helped identify where practices on the job were not united with the standards followed in the training program. This assisted The Select Group to address the discrepancy and make changes across the organization to ensure best practices were followed.

The tests developed for the role are being used to evaluate performance in performance review meetings and aid in promotion decisions. Each section of the course provided a benchmark for success of the required skills. These benchmarks supported the mentors in the organization who worked with poor performers.

By connecting the skills from the course to the metrics within the organization The Select Group was able to confirm a predictive means to adjust the metric. As The Select Group has grown the metrics from each division were monitored and adjusted with the programs. This provided The Select Group with a means to expand quickly and effectively into new offices. The training allowed The Select Group best practices in the recruiter role to be deployed in the new branches in a consistent and easily repeatable manner.

MEASUREMENT FOR COACHING

The process outlined in the ROI by Design™ methodology and detailed in the previous chapters enables effective training design and measurement. Over the past six years, the process has been used by a number of organizations with great success. Companies who have used the methodology for numerous years accumulate a tremendous amount of data on what works and what does not work when addressing performance improvement through training. In addition, these organizations gain the means to predict the effectiveness of training which ensures an increase in performance and enables their employees to meet the demands of new strategic directions.

After using the ROI by Design™ methodology in training for several years with our clients, eParamus™ was presented with a new challenge. A premier consulting firm, The Rowhill Group, approached us with the challenge of measuring the results of one of their coaching engagements. The Rowhill Group specializes in supporting their clients through strategic change. They do this primarily by preparing leaders in the organization to navigate change and exhibit strong leadership skills. In their appointments, they employ strategic advisors, content experts, and professional coaches to address the challenges presented by their clients. For over 12 years they have delivered solutions in the Americas, Africa, Europe, the Middle East, and across Asia Pacific.

For this engagement, the Rowhill team was working with a company from the oil and gas industry that was located in the Middle East. One of Rowhill's main methods for developing the leaders in this organization was through professional coaching. The coaching industry, much like the training industry, does not have a good standard for measurement and therefore rarely completes measurement beyond the perception of impact. However, in this particular instance, before the client would commit to the engagement, they required the Rowhill Group to provide a sound means of measuring the success of leadership change. Jim Sheegog, the principle consultant for The Rowhill Group was aware of the work eParamus™ was doing with measurement in the training industry and contacted us to see if we could help them provide the needed measurement for their coaching.

When first approached with this opportunity, we had to consider how a coaching engagement was similar or dissimilar to training. We knew how well the ROI by Design™ model performed in training but had not yet applied the model to coaching engagements. In considering the differences between coaching and training, we identified two main ways they are different. In the coaching process, we recognized that the coach makes an initial assessment of the person being coached and then develops a plan of areas to address in order to support growth in the individual. This means that in a coaching environment, as opposed to training, you are more likely to be working with an individual instead of a group. In addition, you typically address a variety of areas (those needed for the individual growth) as opposed to one or two subject areas like most training courses.

Outside of these two main differences, the coaching process was very similar to training. There is a planning phase to determine the areas to be covered and the methods to achieve the results. There is an implementation stage where the interventions (coaching sessions) are deployed. Finally, there is a stage after the coaching engagement where the attendee has the opportunity to display the behaviors on the job that they learned and practiced in coaching. In other words there are planning, training (or coaching), transfer, and effectiveness stages where results could be measured.

Once we determined that the stages of evaluation in training were applicable to coaching, we turned our attention to the design of coaching. Understanding that the rigor behind the design of the coaching engagement was the key to the ability to measure coaching, we focused on how a professional coach determines what an individual needs. Once the coach makes that determination, we need to know what methods they use to determine the effectiveness of the results.

We learned that, just like training, coaches use standards (expert knowledge) in their subject areas to determine the objectives when working with an individual. In this case, the main goal was to prepare the organization for strategic change. This required strong leadership. The client requested the support of The Rowhill Group in elevating the competencies of the organization's leaders. The client wanted their leaders to display strong leadership skills that would increase their organization's ability to compete in future markets. The subject for all of the coaching was, in a broad sense, leadership. The Rowhill coaches were well versed in the standards for effective leadership and, although they tailored their coaching for each individual, they addressed leadership with all of the participants. The goal was for all participants to reach a certain level of leadership competency.

This goal required the Rowhill coach to access each leader's current level of leadership so he could customize a plan to reach the desired level. For insistence, one leader may need to work displaying self confidence in his or her leadership position, and another leader may need to work on establishing trust with his or her teams. The Rowhill coaches understood the important areas of leadership and could assess which parts of the leadership competencies were needed for each individual. After assessing the 15 participants, 26 leadership objectives were identified as needed. The number of objectives per participant varied, but participants received their own set of objectives that reflected the areas to be addressed in their coaching meetings.

As the coach identified the leadership areas to address, eParamus™ captured the standards of performance the coach used to benchmark achievement for each objective. With many years of experience, the Rowhill coach combined several different works from leadership experts such as Jack Canfield, Jim Collins, and John Maxwell to create the objectives. For each objective, standards of performance were identified. The standards were translated into the leadership behaviors that reflected the acquisition of the leadership standard. The objectives and subsequent standards were used by the coach (and the organization) to be confident that the participant mastered the level of leadership competency required.

The identification of objectives and standards (in terms of behaviors) became the benchmarks used for measurement. Like training, a pre-test, post-test, and transfer assessment could be made using these standards. The standards supported the level two (learning) and level three (behavior change) measurements we needed. However, to reach the level four (results) measurements, we needed to categorize the different objectives to allow for a combination of objectives to have an impact on company metrics. In most training programs, determining the metric is much easier because training is typically requested when there is a performance gap or a performance need in the organization. When training is requested, there is usually an indicator (metric) that can be monitored to identify organizational results. Training programs naturally address certain subjects, leading to certain behaviors, and certain outcomes. In this case, the organization needed to identify the metrics that were influenced by a variety of leadership competencies because the coaching was customized for each leader. This presented us with a new challenge.

To address the challenge of determining metrics for a level four assessment, we categorized the leadership objectives into groups. Since all of the objectives addressed leadership, we were able to group the objectives by three main leadership competencies. The three main areas to emerge were emotional intelligence, interpersonal mastery, and alignment to future. The emotional intelligence area included objectives that addressed a leader's strength of self. When leaders do not have a strong sense of self, they are less likely to have confidence in their ability to lead and will often refrain from developing plans and directing their teams. The interpersonal mastery area included objectives that addressed the ability of leaders to motivate and develop their teams as well as influence their peers. When a leaders lack interpersonal mastery, they struggle with building team unity. This often translates into low productivity of the teams they lead. The final area was alignment to future. The alignment to future area addressed objectives that reflected the ability of leaders to problem solve and to drive the organization strategically. Leaders who are proficient in this area often have a reduction in problems or a quicker resolution to problems.

By categorizing leadership into these three main areas we drew conclusions on expected organizational impact. The impact to the organization was not reflected in the individual objectives but instead in the combination of objectives addressing a particular competency area. This was achieved because particular competencies lead to skills and abilities. Skills and abilities lead to outputs. When objectives for the leaders were combined, clear evidence of the achievement of those objectives could be realized. Measurement of level four was made by comparing the impact to the identified metrics for the leaders prior to the program as opposed to after the program. In addition, since there were several groups of leaders who were going through the coaching at different times, a comparison of metrics between the leaders who completed the program and those who had not could be made.

Conclusion

Both training and coaching are methods used to develop employees and improve productivity in organizations. Both training and coaching can be effective in moving an organization forward by fostering new knowledge, skills, and abilities. The central components of training that allow it to be effective and measurable are present in coaching. Both training and coaching employ the same basic components and processes and therefore can be measured, evaluated, and improved using the same methods.

The individualistic nature of a coaching engagement allowed for a concentrated effort on individual objectives and the combination of objectives supported real impact to organizational outputs. Like training, during the implementation of the coaching program we were able to monitor the success of each stage of the process and provide intervention when the gains were not as expected. In addition, at the completion of the coaching engagement, we were able to produce the same detailed reports used in training measurement, showing the acquisition and the application of behaviors covered in the objectives.

The ROI by Design™ model of evaluation transferred well into the coaching environment. The components used to induce rigor in training design were easily incorporated into the design for the coaching engagement. In fact, since coaching and training are both methods that support the acquisition of knowledge, skills, and abilities, the barriers to acquisition and application were strikingly similar (as were their repairs)! Companies who prefer to use coaching methods to support the development of their employees and leaders can incorporate measurement in order to evaluate their results, repair barriers to success, and capture the impact coaching has on their organization.

AFTERWORD

To this point, we have reviewed the state of the training industry, and identified the need for a new impact evaluation method. We have detailed specific best practices in instructional design that qualify for measurement, and described an impact model to evaluate student learning, as well as the process of training and its application within an organization. We have described the results this model provides both for organizations and the training industry as a whole. We have reviewed how this same model can apply to both coaching and training.

The most important questions now are these: If you take the lessons learned and apply them to your organization, what will you get? Will the training profession and your organization benefit? Will the results be worth it? Will it make your work better?

Let's start with that first question. If you take the lessons learned from this book and apply them to your organization, what will you get? You will be able to identify the important behaviors in your organization that impact effectiveness and profitability. You will be able to tie those behaviors to specific and measurable metrics. Knowing how the behavior ties to the metric and how training impacts both behavior and metrics, you will be able to achieve repeatable and consistent outcomes for your training. Additionally, use of the ROI by Design™ model will result in the establishment of a common language and better, more effective collaboration between trainers and business unit managers. Your role will become clearer to you and to your organization. You will be able to point to the specific impact your training programs have made on the organization. Training requesters will understand your level of expertise and will defer to you for training design decisions.

Will the training profession and your organization benefit? The answer is a resounding yes! You will help transform the notion that training is an ambiguous, amorphous practice that cannot be measured. The impact model will show in concrete terms both the value of the training profession and how that value translates directly to bottom-line dollars for your organization.

Will the results be worth it and will it make your work better? Again, the answer is a resounding yes! Perhaps that answer will become clearer the first time you go through the budget process and don't have to fight tooth and nail for every dollar received. Or when, for the first time, the executives in charge of your budget no longer consider training a "nice to have" but rather a "must have."

It is possible to transform our industry. We can become a strategic business partner once we understand our value. We must know how to communicate that value in business terms—as dollars and cents, as hard proof of achieved goals that add to the bottom line. The key to all of it is accurate, results-driven training design and measurement. The ROI by Design™ model is the answer.

ABOUT THE AUTHOR

Laura Paramoure, EdD, has more than 25 years of academic and private sector experience in organizational development, training measurement, and training design. She conducted primary research to develop thought leadership on training effectiveness and measurement culminating in her dissertation *Perceptions of training and non-training managers of organizational impact measures based on design intent.* She also authored *Showing Value for Your Training Dollars.* Dr. Paramoure regularly speaks about training ROI at seminars for organizations such as American Society of Training and Development (ASTD) and International Society of Performance Improvement (ISPI). She is currently President and CEO of eParamus™ (www.eparamus.com), a company that helps organizations of all types and sizes determine the dollar value and ROI of their training programs.

To contact eParamus about your training needs call 919.882.2108 or email info@eparamus.com.

Made in the USA
San Bernardino, CA
14 December 2016